Purple Turtle

BABY RECORD BOOK

This book has
precious memories of

----

as a baby.

A Star is BORN

My name is

_____

♥ was **i BORN** on

_____

Time of **ARRIVAL**

♥ was **i BORN** at

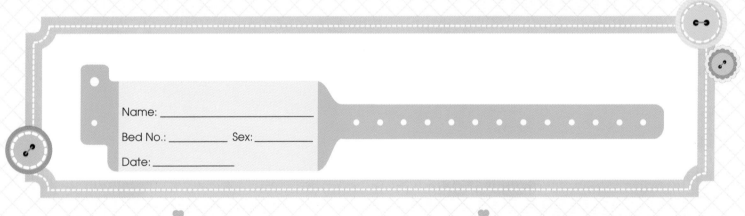

Name: _____

Bed No.: _____ Sex: _____

Date: _____

i weighed   **i** measured

_____

My blood group is   **My** hair was   **My** eyes were

_____

MAGICAL Moments

Paste an envelope to hold the
birth certificate

Paste photo here

My first photo

My **FIRST** PHOTOS

Paste photo here

Me and my mama

Place scan here

Paste photo here

Me and my papa

My FIRST VISITORS

Paste photo here

My first visitors were

They said I looked like

My New HOME

i left
hospital **ON**

....

My first address

....
....
....
....

FIRST Fun MOMENTS

My first fun bath was on

- -

- -

My favourite bath toys were

- -

- -

Paste photo here

My **NAMING** Ceremony

i was named by

Paste photo here

Paste photo here

i was named on

in the presence of

Sweet
DREAMS

Paste photo here

Sleep Pattern

Age	Sleeping needs
New borns (0 - 2 months)	12 to 18 hrs
Infants (3 - 11 months)	14 to 15 hrs
Toddlers (1 - 3 years)	12 to 14 hrs

I woke up

_____ times

every night untill I was

_____

months old.

Paste photo here

My Little FINGERS

Place baby's handprint

My Little TOES

Place baby's footprint

My FIRST

Yummy FOODS

- - - - - - - - - - - - - -

- - - - - - - - - - - - - -

- - - - - - - - - - - - - -

- - - - - - - - - - - - - -

Yucky FOODS

- - - - - - - - - - - - - -

- - - - - - - - - - - - - -

- - - - - - - - - - - - - -

- - - - - - - - - - - - - -

Paste photo here

F O O D

Yummy FOODS

Paste photo here

Paste photo here

Yucky FOODS

Paste photo here

My **FIRST OUTING**

On _____

I went to _____

With _____

_____

My FIRST Set of MILK TEETH

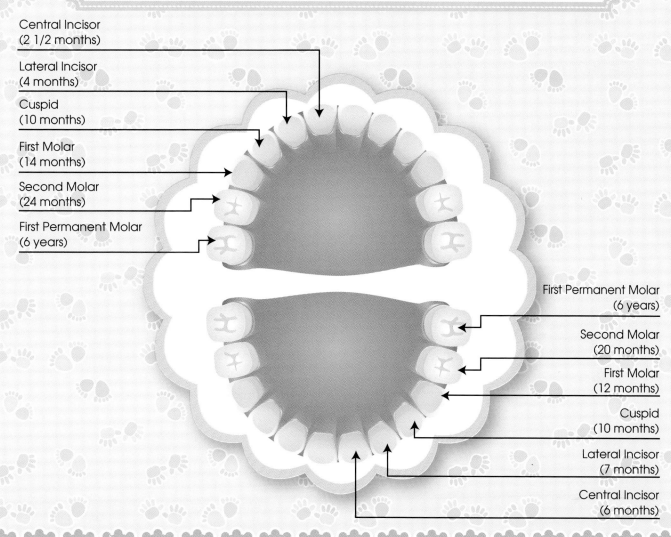

Central Incisor
(2 1/2 months)

Lateral Incisor
(4 months)

Cuspid
(10 months)

First Molar
(14 months)

Second Molar
(24 months)

First Permanent Molar
(6 years)

First Permanent Molar
(6 years)

Second Molar
(20 months)

First Molar
(12 months)

Cuspid
(10 months)

Lateral Incisor
(7 months)

Central Incisor
(6 months)

Date of my first visit ....

Dentist's name ....

Memories of my first visit ....

My FIRST
hair cut

(Before haircut)
Paste photo here

(After haircut)
Paste photo here

Paste an envelope to store the
baby's first lock of hair.

My CUTIE-PIE Moves

First sat

First crawled

First stood

First walked

Paste photo here

Paste photo here

Paste photo here

Paste photo here

Paste photo here

My first birthday

was celebrated at

- - - - - - - - - - - - - - - - -

Gifts I received

- - - - - - - - - - - - - - - - -

My MILESTONES

At one month

Paste photo here

At two months

Paste photo here

At three months

Paste photo here

At four months

Paste photo here

At five months

Paste photo here

At six months

Paste photo here

WATCH me GROW

At seven months

Paste photo here

At eight months

Paste photo here

At nine months

Paste photo here

At ten months

Paste photo here

At eleven months

Paste photo here

At twelve months

Paste photo here

My FIRST HOLIDAY

DATE

_____

i went
with _____

WE
went to _____

WE
had fun _____

_____

_____

Paste photo here

Paste photo here

My FIRST Drawing

Paste drawing here

I was only

_ _

old when I drew this masterpiece.

Color Pencil

MY
Sweetest
SMILE

Paste photo here

Paste photo here

Paste photo here

My VACCINATIONS

Paste photo here

Paste photo here

Vaccinations I have had   **D**ate

My FIRST
FRIENDS

Paste photo here

Paste photo here

Paste photo here

My **FAVOURITE** **THINGS**

Paste photo here

Paste photo here

Toy _____

Book _____

Activity _____

Game _____

Rhyme _____

Story _____

My FAMILY Photo

Paste photo here

This photo of my family
was taken on

My GROWTH Chart

Age	Weight	Height
One week		
Two weeks		
One month		
Two months		
Three months		
Four months		
Five months		
Six months		
Seven months		
Eight months		
Nine months		
Ten months		
Eleven months		
One year		

Paste photo here

Paste photo here